Ivan

MW01296069

THE
MOON

MAGNET
FOR THE SOUL

SAMKHYA PUBLISHING LTD
London, 2020

Translated by
Milica Breber

Proofreading & editing by
James Joshua Pennington, PhD

Book cover design by
Zoran Ignjatovic
https://ignjatoviczoran.weebly.com

TABLE OF CONTENTS

Introduction 5

Unknown facts about the Moon 8

The story of incarnation of human souls and why
they happen 17

The influence of the Moon on the soul 28

The position of the Moon in cosmic proportions 33

Solar and lunar cults 38

The influence of the Moon in astropsychology 40

Lilith – The Black Moon – That, too, exists 50

The Moon and the polarization of humans 52

Liberation from the influence of the Moon 55

And finally, who framed us with the Moon 69

INTRODUCTION

Ancient traditions that originated on African and Asian soil, seem to suggest that not so long ago there was no Moon in the sky as our companion, and life on planet Earth was completely different. There were no seasons then, and the climate was temperate and very pleasant all round the globe, with mild mist and luscious greenery. We often hear folklore of the 'golden age' when humans lived in harmony with nature and himself, with a much greater perceptive ability than they have today. It was all changed about 12.000 years ago when near cataclysmic events took place on Earth. These changes modern biological and geological studies confirm. Climate suffered a terrible change, poles shifted, ocean levels rose, great floods wreaked havoc on Earth and ... the Moon showed up.

Let us see, first of all, what we know about the Moon. Upon close inspection we come to realize that we know almost nothing, that all the generally accepted information regarding the Moon is illogical and not substantiated by evidence. Then, we take a closer look at the scarce data we have and things which are completely unknown about the Moon, from the viewpoint of esoteric tradition, astrology and information that reached us from very distant sources, from the stellar systems of Sirius and Pleiades. Namely, if the Moon appeared all of a sudden in our night sky one day, somebody had to bring it here and strategically set its erratic, unnatural movement. Part of the information in this book comes from those who engineered such a feat. The other part of information comes from our scientists who have no problem to observe objectively and accurately the object of research, in this case the Moon. Their scientific research has shown that the Moon was artificially constructed and put in orbit. Later, we discover how all this information perfectly adds up even though the sources they come from differ greatly.

The obvious conclusion is that if the Moon is not Earth's natural satellite but an artificial body, the extra-terrestrial intervention is also necessary. It is hardly a problem for me to accept this since I have had three encounters with them so far. It poses a problem, however, for those who have never had a personal experience with them. They can do nothing else but believe that 'we are not alone' to a degree their courage and freedom of thought permits them, to think out of the box and beyond the standards imposed by public opinion.

Likewise, if we look at the influence of the Moon on a human's soul, we must take into account the idea of reincarnation and soul. Those topics are also not new to me. After 40 odd years of meditative practice and out-of-body experiences, including the experiences with dead people, I have personally come to be assured of the reality of incarnations and the relationship between the mind in the body and the higher consciousness of the soul.

We not only deal with the cosmological aspect of the Moon here, but its psychological and astrological influence, as well. I have studied astrology for a great many years and monitored its impact in practice not only on me, but on all the people around me. Understanding the Moon without astrology is a dead-end; it leads nowhere.

Therefore, the main topic here is the influence of the Moon on the incarnation cycle of our souls, why there is the Moon in our sky in the first place, and how it affects our lives and soul. In order to understand that, we must firstly know how it came about that it exists there where it is, together with all the cosmological details of the Moon. Afterward, it becomes clear to us why it exists.

Namely, we see that it is impossible to know the truth about the Moon if the issue of its existence is kept apart form its influence on humans, and the influence on humans cannot be separated from the issue of incarnation and soul. Hence, the story of the Moon does not merely refer to it, it is inseparable from the purpose of the origin of humankind and the secret of human soul, and the reason why it is born in this world.

The old wise men kept telling us that the heaven and the earth come together in humans. Modern wise men confirm this, pointing to the fact that everything is interconnected in the holographic universe.

UNKNOWN FACTS ABOUT THE MOON

Science only provides us with the theory according to which the Moon is a natural celestial body, the Earth's satellite, which probably originated after some body the size of Mars hit the Earth about 4 billion years ago, knocked off a huge chunk of its mass which became the Moon as we know it today. Naturally, there is not a shred of evidence to support this theory. Everything else we know about the Moon confirms the words of Irwin Shapiro, from the Harvard-Smithsonian center for astrophysics: "The best explanation about the Moon is: 'observational error' – the Moon should not exists at all."

Its composition and movement are unnatural.

The oldest rock formations on the Moon precede those on the Earth by a billion years. The chemical components of the Moon's soil are significantly different from the ones we have on Earth, more than anything because of the large quantity of helium 3, which lacks on Earth.

The movement of the Moon is a story in itself which further goes to prove its unnaturality.

The Moon is 400 times smaller than the Sun, and during the eclipse it is 400 times closer to the Earth than the Sun. That is the reason why the Moon during the solar eclipse, observed from the Earth, is the same size like the Sun because there is total eclipse. To cut a long story short, the Moon is in perfect synchronicity with the Sun. This is impossible in natural phenomena. The Moon always keeps showing the same side toward the Earth.

This is also impossible in natural phenomena because they are always changeable. We can never see the dark side of the Moon due to the perfect synchronicity of the Moon's rotation. If the diameter of the Moon is multiplied in the ratio of the Earth, the result is 436.669.140 kilometers. If this number is divided by 100 it becomes 436.669 km which is the diameter of the Sun with the precision of 99.9 per cent. If you divide the diameter of the Sun in the ratio of the Moon you get the diameter of the Earth. Divide the size of the Sun and the size of the Earth and multiply it by 100 and you get the size of the Moon.

The ratio of the Sun, Moon and Earth is based on natural mathematics, on the Fibonacci sequence (golden section, 1:1,618) everything in nature is based on, and all the proportions of growth. It was done in such a way because the Moon generates evolution of consciousness on the Earth.

The assumption of the Moon as a gigantic space ship was put forth in July 1970. by Mikhail Vasin and Alexander Shcherbakov, two members of the Soviet academy of sciences. In the Soviet magazine Sputnik they published an article titled *"Is the Moon the Creation of Alien Intelligence?"* They stated that the Moon is a planetoid hollowed out with the help of extremely advanced technology used to melt the rock and create indentation in its interior. Afterward, this 'metallic, stony debris' was poured out making the lunar surface the way we know it today.

Dr. D. L. Anderson, a professor of geophysics and director of seismological laboratory at the California Institute of Technology once said that "Moon was made inside out." Its inner and outer crust go to suggest that they should be placed in reverse.

Several spacecraft were sent to perform the experiments and find out if the Moon were a hollow object. After NASA placed seismometers on the Moon a few spacecraft were launched with the goal of crashing onto the Moon's surface. This provided additional results that backed the claim of the Moon being a hollow body. Impact equaling a ton of TNT set off shock waves that kept on spreading for eight minutes, and in the words of a NASA scientist, the Moon 'rang like a bell'. "It was as though somebody struck the church bell once, only to discover that the ringing lasts for 30 minutes more." The Moon was later subjected to an explosion that equaled eleven tons of TNT when the launch vehicle Sat-urn V was crashed onto its surface after an aborted mission. The Moon then 'reacted like a gong', NASA scientists confirmed, and the vibrations that penetrated as deep as 40 kilometers into the ground lasted for three hours and twenty minutes. Alan Butler, co-author of the book "*Who Built the Moon?*" (Christopher Knight and Alan Butler) spoke about it with Ken Johnson, director of the department for the data and photo control during the Apollo missions. Johnson said that the Moon did not only ring like a bell. He said that the entire Moon was "shaking" in such a precise manner that "it looked like it had gigantic hydraulic vibration silencers inside."

Something was found on the Moon that should not be there, at all: uranium 236 and neptunium 237. The Soviet scientists Vasin and Shcherbakov stated that the presence of these elements can be explained by an assumption that nuclear energy was used for drilling out the Moon, and those might well be the remains of construction on the Moon. These are radioactive elements, byproducts of the nuclear reactors and plutonium production, uranium 236 is a radioactive nuclear waste from used fuel and reprocessed uranium. They do not exist in nature. What are they doing there if the Moon is a 'natural' celestial body?

Unexplained activity on the surface of the Moon is constantly revealed and concealed. Numerous UFO phenomena on and around the Moon are a special area of interest among ufologists and astronomers alike. Ex NASA workers and people who follow their work mention the removal of unnatural phenomena from the Moon photos before the public get the chance to see them. Sergeant Karl Wolfe worked as a precision electronics photograph technician at (CIA) Langley Air Force Base in Virginia. On one conference at the National Press Club in Washington, D.C. in 2001 Wolf testified to photos he had seen of huge buildings on the more remote side of the Moon taken in 1965. He explains that he was assigned to resolve a technical glitch in the part of base where they pieced together something like a mosaic of photos taken on the Moon in order to come up with a bigger picture. Wolfe added how a pilot who was in charge of the photos said: "By the way, on the backside of the Moon we discovered a base of some kind." He then proceeded to show him the photo of the base in question with various geometric shapes, spherical buildings, very tall towers and something that looked like radar dishes. Some structures had reflecting surfaces, and others reminded him of cooling towers in power plant. Some of the towers were flat and tall, with a sawed-off top, or spherical in shape and resembling a dome. He stressed that many of these constructions were huge. Some of the constructions measured at least 800 meters in height.

Richard Hoagland, an ex photography expert at NASA brings forth evidence that the Moon is full of buildings and how NASA concealed and fixed reports and pictures. He revealed that there are huge glass constructions for purposes unknown, on the Moon and around it. Glass which is made in airless space is many times stronger than steel, there are no air bubbles that make it weak, which makes it the perfect building material, and is barely visible in space.

There are testimonies of cosmonauts who sighted extraterrestrial activities on the Moon, and managed to record some of them. And yes, they went on the Moon. However, since going to the Moon was part of the state propaganda during the cold war, the entire event had to receive a lot of media coverage, Apollo mission was turned into a televised show for the whole nation, orchestrated by top Hollywood and Disney moguls. They desperately needed direct broadcast of the Moon landing, but they were not technologically well-equipped for that at the time. If they could not produce one good shot it is like they never went there. Cameras could not tape landing outside the module, on the Moon, because a huge difference in temperature would deform the lenses, film and the entire camera (in the space of two hours the temperature would go from plus 130 degrees Celsius to minus 150 degrees Celsius). Only one tiny part was filmed, the moment of landing, from the inside of the module. Hence, the entire landing scene on the Moon's surface had to be shot in the studio. Donald Rumsfeld suggested director Stanley Kubrick for the job, in the studio in London where the *Odyssey 2001* was made. Kubrick later asked for a return favor from NASA to loan a special new lens for filming in low light, such as candle light, which he used in the making of his next picture, *Barry Lyndon*, 1975. It was a unique lens with Zeiss lens for spy satellites, very valuable and safeguarded as state secret. All of this was confirmed by the participants of this event, Henry Kissinger, head of the CIA at that time Richard Helms, USA government ministers of the era, Donald Rumsfeld, Alexander Haig, counselor Lawrence Eagleburger, Stanley Kubrick's wife, Christiane Kubrick in the William Karel's documentary *Opération Lune*. According to their testimony, to ensure that everything remains a secret, CIA killed all the technicians who made the recording. Kubrick was spared, but he feared for his life and never left his estate.

So, the flight to the Moon really happened, they were there, only recordings of this flight were filmed mostly on Earth, because there was no technology to make them on the Moon. Later Apollo missions had the real shots. The background of the whole project was the development of rocket technology for the intercontinental ballistic missile, and not a walk on the Moon.

To keep all the activities and anomalies on the Moon secret today, hidden away from the many observers and amateur astronomers, it seems that the surface of the Moon we see is not its real surface. There is a possibility that a holographic image is projected onto the surface which shows the Moon as being always the same. This doubt originated after a careful observation of the pictures of the Moon's surface taken through a telescope, where a wave descending horizontally at precise intervals can be seen, which appears to enable the holographic image to follow the movement of the Moon. Many astronomers in the world who observe the Moon testify to the same.[1]

---

[1] For more on this see the you tube footage: 9 Lunar Waves Filmed - Game Change
https://www.youtube.com/watch?v=0mi0w8bLtUM

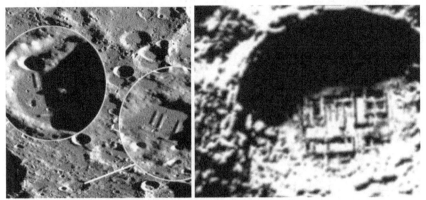

Remains of construction on the Moon

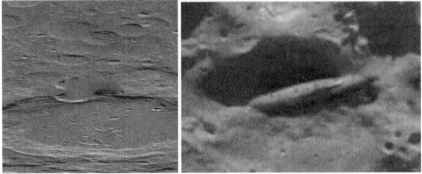

Object on the Moon smudged out on NASA photo

Alien spaceship on the Moon, Picture taken by Apollo 15, 17, 20

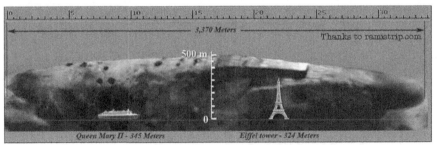

3,370 Meters

Thanks to ramstrip.com

500 m

Queen Mary II - 345 Meters

Eiffel tower - 324 Meters

Dimensions of an alien spaceship on the Moon

Therefore, we see the next logical coherence: evidence that the Moon is not a natural celestial body prove the involvement of some advanced alien force, because it is not man-made. We cannot stop at the sheer wealth of evidence of the Moon being an artificial creation without accepting alien intervention. Together with all of this, we must conclude that human life on this planet was planned a long time ago before people, and not only by the people.

Moon being an artificial creation should not shock us too much because the confirmation that consciousness is at the base of all the creation we have in us and all around us, in all the scientific facts.[2] Our DNA is also an artificial creation, a work of intelligent design. Scientists calculated that cosmos is not old enough to enable the creation of DNA or any other cell simply by random particle collision. Cambridge University astrophysicist Fred Hoyle had this to say on the subject:' 'The likelihood of a living cell arising through evolution is the same as a tornado sweeping through a junkyard and assembling a Boeing 747."

We should not be afraid that some great intelligent superpower made such a huge thing like the Moon is, to trick us into thinking this world is nothing but a *Truman show*.[3] **Consciousness that did all of this is actually our own consciousness**, we only use it to a much smaller per cent, and there is a reason that justifies that. There are not multitudes of consciousnesses, it is one and the same in everything, it only divides itself and branches out into all the possible individual shapes. Our incarnations are among the many individual shapes. Therefore,

---

[2] For more on this see the work by Stephen Meyer: *Signature in the Cell: DNA and the Evidence for Intelligent Design*, and the work of the Nobel prize winner Francis Crick: Life Itself: Its Origin and Nature.
[3] Film *The Truman Show*, 1998.

to be able to understand the nature of consciousness that created the Moon and the reason why it was done we must begin with understanding ourselves first, and we can never really understand ourselves without understanding our incarnations. Only by accepting reincarnation, at least theoretically, is it possible to understand the human nature and together with it the nature of this world, the entire solar system. If the Earth and the Moon make one big stage, then it is clear that it was set for the actors, *for us*, more accurately for us to play our karmic drama during the incarnation cycle.

With such understanding of the true nature of divine consciousness which we are a very important part of, as well, this world with the Moon is a lot more wondrous and beautiful than when we were admiring the moonlight dreaming of all sorts of things.

THE STORY OF THE INCARNATION OF HUMAN SOULS AND WHY THEY HAPPEN

In order to understand the reason why there is incarnation of the souls, we must firstly get acquainted with the very notion of the soul, and what it truly is. It is a reflection of divine consciousness or the Absolute which is everything that exists. Our essence or soul is an individual emanation of the absolute divine consciousness, which is all that is. (What else could it be?)[4]

According to an ancient parable, the manifestation of the divine consciousness and human soul can best be understood if we picture a tree whose roots are in the sky and branches with leaves are on the ground (reality is, by the way, reverse to a large degree from our perception). Divine consciousness is a root in the highest sky, on the highest dimension, ether or *akasha*, known to us as the quantum field, universal field in modern termi-

---

[4] *Advaita vedanta* is based on the saying: This *atman* (our soul) is *brahman* (Absolute, everything-that-is). It is you (*Tat tvam asi*).
Darshana-upanishad (X, 10): "When all the beings we see in their own Self (soul), and in all the beings we see the Self (soul), then *brahman* (divine) we attain."

In *Katha upanishad* (II, 1.10) it is said: "What is here is also there; what is there, also here. Who sees multiplicity but not the one indivisible Self must wander on and on from death to death." This is a description of the reality of holographic universe. We cannot be any different from it, we can be and we are its conscious subjects. However, we have the freedom to imagine everything, even that we are different and separate from it.

nology, in which in implicit and timeless order exists everything that has ever manifested in duration over a period of time. From the divine consciousness of the Absolute the consciousness of itself is manifested, firstly in the form of monad resembling the tree trunk. Together with it the manifestation of cosmos was set in motion. First bigger monads of consciousness start to branch out from that point onward. In religious and mystical experience they are known as the archangels and seraphim. In the physical cosmos entities the size of galaxies correspond to them. They further branch out in an ever finer way as lower monads of consciousness known to us as angels in religion and mysticism. In the physical cosmos stars and their planetary systems correspond to them. On our tree those would be the branches with leaves on them. The tiniest branches that have special groups of leaves would be the over-souls, the big souls that further split into individual souls into individual physical bodies. They would correspond to leaves in our parable.

Individual souls are divided into the young buds, mature souls or blossoms, and old souls that are the fruits of our tree of life. Old and the most mature souls who are aware of this process and recognize the whole tree of life in themselves, represent its seed or essence. In the seed the whole tree is present in its holographic shape. When it submits itself to the divine whole, to its essence, when it 'dies', it disappears as an individual and becomes the divine whole all over again. It is important to stress here that all the souls are the same and equally timeless, only under the illusion of linear time of the physical world it appears as though some of them are young and some are old, which merely depends on their experience in the cycle of incarnations. Every soul has multiple incarnations, those beginning its cycle are young, still adjusting to the world, and those that are ending it are old in the sense that they have gathered enough experience and have got to know the world in its entirety. We can see the same in our experience with people, some are born intelligent and wise, they are aware of the meaning of things straight away, while others bother to learn a little bit about life only when they are forced to do so, but mostly attain nothing; some are good and compassionate, and some are negative and destructive. It is all due to the karmic maturity of the souls. This maturity determines the level of consciousness and emotional maturity, as well. All the conflicts between people happen because of the different levels of consciousness, that is the different karmic maturity of the soul, and all the harmonious relationships are a consequence of the compatibility of those levels.

In this whole process there is one universal rule: divine consciousness, the one which is everything-that-is, manifests itself and everything-that-can-be. When an individual soul experiences everything-that-can-be, it retrieves this consciousness to the divine Absolute. In this way it realizes its completeness through manifestation in existence.

Divine consciousness manifests itself firstly as the elementary form of particles, atoms, molecules and all their possible shapes. When elementary shapes finalize all their possibilities, a higher form of manifestation of divine consciousness is developed, which is plant life, and the perception develops in them. Plants experience all the possible forms of adjusting to the environment for the sake of survival. By doing so they develop basic perception of physical bodies. Higher form of perception develops in animal bodies. They not only perceive, but move as well, and the divine consciousness manifests itself through movement and perception, through developing all the survival skills on the level of movement and perception. It is achieved through the laws of survival and food chain. Perception in animals gets perfected under pressure of hunter and prey competitiveness. In order to survive both parties must upgrade their abilities. At long last, a being with the most perfect sensory and activity organs and complete perception is born: the man himself. Only man has all the sensory and activity organs perfected well enough so that he does not only survive, but create new value, he reach the meaning of existence. In man's life existence overcomes the phase of movement for the sake of survival and crosses over to understanding the meaning of survival and existence in general. It is the purpose of human actions or karma: understanding the meaning. All human drama is brought about because of the struggle to make sense of our existence. We all search for understanding in this world in all ways available to us, in the relationships with other people and regarding the existence itself. Existence gets its dramatic character through man, it ceases to be sheer survival. However, this drama is tragedy and comedy all in one. It is play and beauty, creativity and art, joy and suffering, wandering through a series of mistakes, and the joy of revelation, it is everything-that-can-be, experiencing everything and all the human possibilities. Above all, it leads to **understanding** the soul which a man in this game offers to man, to his dear one, to himself, the understanding of the consciousness of divine soul which is trapped in the body and limited by the physical mind and ego.

This entire odyssey of divine Absolute through the highest monads of creative consciousness, and through the entire nature and all the human life dramas, as its startup force, aside from inspiration which originates from the very divine consciousness as the source of everything, must also have coercion and pressure to make it grow. The problem is in the following: a human's soul is of divine origin, its awareness of itself is always self-sufficient. Whoever has come to know their soul is aware of the divine presence in the very existence, in the overall existence. He no longer sees the difference between existence and divine consciousness that is at the base of existence, the same way they no longer see the difference between their consciousness and the divine consciousness. It is all the same to them. This is how they view reality. But they then stop their growth on the physical plane. They lack motivation to work and develop life through their physical body, because they have known what constitutes the body, and that is so much higher and more valuable. There is the mesmerizing feeling of bliss once we raise the awareness of reality (*sat-chit-ananda* – reality/is/consciousness/is/bliss). Many cases of saints who, after a personal experience of God-knowing, choose to live very humble lives, in caves and without any financial means of any kind, are the perfect illustration for this. To them it is enough, but it is not good for economy and the technological progress which is planned for planet Earth. ***This is why souls in the body need coercion to be made to work and create. This coercion is received with the aid of the Moon.***

What did human souls do before the Earth and how did they come to Earth?

There are two ways in which to address this issue – through ***the individual and collective plane***.

From the individual perspective, human souls before their arrival on Earth created all the living world that would exist on planet Earth, all the living conditions, all the plant and animal life, they are all a product of intelligent design of our souls before their incarnation into the physical body. There is evidence from hypnotic regression that we preplanned our lives before being born even. That is not the complete picture, though. Not only did we plan the main roads and motives of our life dramas in the body, but we created this body, and in order to be able to create it, we had to create all the living conditions for this body to live in prior to that. The ground we stand on, the air we breathe, water, the food we eat, it is all a product of intelligent design of the consciousness of our souls from the higher dimensions.

In order to understand the collective plane we must rely on the alternative history of humankind. This official history being taught by the mainstream academia informs us that we originated from the apes accidentally, we have made a little physical progress since then, but on the inside we have become worse than apes because we threaten to destroy the planet with our own stupidity. Not even the apes would do that. Naturally, scientists making these outrageous claims conveniently forget to tell us that the planet is not being polluted by people, but by corporations. They, themselves, are on the payroll of these corporations. There are about 43.000 corporations worldwide. Upon a close inspection, when we track down their joint capital and managerial positions we can see that the number barely exceeds 400, most of which are, through cross ownership and CEO's, controlled by about 20 banks. The owners of the banks in question are several aristocratic families. In this way they control all the modern living and the whole world, including science and education. They keep forcing us to run on oil and electricity instead of hydrogen and fuel cells.[5] This is why they call us apes.[6]

According to the esoteric, alternative history of humankind, we are star seed. *From the collective perspective*, human souls did not incarnate in the physical bodies on Earth for the first time, they had already descended in this galaxy before that, in this physical universe in the constellation of Lyra. There they started to experience the charm of physical survival step by step. The charm was this: in the divine Absolute everything is one, no differentiations, therefore no experiences. In order for the divine consciousness, which is everything-that-is, to manifest itself as everything-that-can-be, a physical universe of some kind was required, within the boundaries of the linear time and space where everything is divided and available for all kinds of experiences, from all the aspects and with enough repetitions. In higher dimensions this is not an option.

When through the individual souls it experiences everything-that-is, then the divine consciousness goes back to itself, it recognizes itself in everything that is. This completes the manifestation of the divine Absolute in its entirety. Then the cycle of incarnations of an individual soul ends.

---

[5] A recent study in Germany showed that the electric propulsion in a car, available today, is ecologically and economically more harmful than diesel propulsion.

[6] Although there is a full-blown conspiracy against people by the elite, so successfully uncovered by David Icke, it serves the same purpose as the Moon does: to introduce the necessary pressure for the people to wake up. Never have people been more aware of themselves and their position than today, when the conspiracy against the people and human liberties is the biggest. It all has a positive effect even though it appears negative.

However, as we have stated before, souls are self-sufficient and they cannot make the full circle and go through all the experiences on their own, especially the ones that include all the oppositions, good and evil. Souls are the manifestation of pure good and divine perfection, that is why they cannot generate evil in order to experience it. It has to come from the outside. And so it did. The very divine Absolute saw to it that, apart from the monads of divine souls, it manifested certain conscious entities that are not in possession of its consciousness of itself, which do not find their identity in the human form as human souls. They are so-called Satanic, Luciferian or demonic forces. Of all the manifestations of divine consciousness **human souls make up for two thirds of the manifested, and the inhuman entities without a soul make up for the remaining third**. It works this way because in order to overcome the evil and destructive, it takes double the strength of the good and constructive. To put it in religious terms, divine consciousness created one third evil and demonic forces, and two thirds of the good and angelic ones, that our souls originate from. These negative forces exist to exert the necessary pressure and the much needed coercion on human souls, to make them experience all the aspects of existence in all the oppositions that souls would never be able to experience on their own. These are the so-called evil or negative experiences. It is required because on the physical plane consciousness is crystallized through all the possible experiences, the experiences of oppositions included.

When human souls materialized to a sufficient degree in the constellation of Lyra, with all the divine powers in their physical bodies, the negative forces came and started an open conflict against them. It happened in order to make the souls migrate from the constellation of Lyra to all the other constellations, the Pleiades, Tau Ceti, Aldebaran, Orion…. The more they spread and multiplied in a perpetual conflict with the negative forces, they more and more declined into material conditioning, everything they had and new came from their memory of their background and origin in Lyra. Nothing more than a myth remained and the conflicts grew stronger, even the ones amongst themselves. The last stop of their colonization was on Mars and planet Maldek (or Phaeton), which orbited between Mars and Jupiter. Negative forces attacked them there, as well, destroyed planet Maldek and the aftermath is just an asteroid belt visible in the sky,[7] they then devastated Mars which still has traces of nuclear radiation on it, and most importantly, Mars and the Earth swapped positions, that is orbits, and ultimately the Earth became a better planet to live on. People moved from Mars and

---

[7] NASA sent a probe into the asteroid belt and proved there are remains of a planet that orbited a long time ago between Mars and Jupiter. Besides, according to Titius-Bode law, orbits of all the planets in the solar system are at an equal distance away from the Sun, the only exception is that between Mars and Jupiter there is double the required space suggesting that there must have been a planet there in the past. However, we must suspect the honesty of NASA who after this research did not make the effort to explain how this planet disappeared. Who crashed this planet? Darth Vader? There is a similar claim regarding Mars where they openly admit it had seas and rivers, but do not attempt to solve the mystery as to where they had all gone and how. Any lay person knows that it takes an event of cataclysmic proportions and the change in planet's orbit. Such catastrophes with Mars and the destruction of Maldek cannot be natural phenomena, because planets do not change their orbit suddenly, especially not only one in a finely tuned system, they do not go around in space crashing into one another, and in such a way that only one gets destroyed in the collision.

Maldek to Earth, on Atlantis, Sumer, the Indus Valley, Caucasus and Balkan.

For many a century they lived on the Earth owing to their ancient knowledge in cosmology and science, all the megalithic mega structures were engineered back then containing all the cosmological knowledge that cannot be acquired by simple observation from the Earth (precession), whereas their intriguing feats of engineering are impossible to replicate even today. Cosmic technology is necessary to be used for such super buildings. This idyll lasted up until 12.000 years B.C. It was not all so ideal up until then, either. On the part of landmass known as Atlantis to us today people degenerated into one-sidedness and distanced themselves form spirituality, they started to abuse their technological advancements to satisfy their lowest goals. Non-human entities infiltrated themselves into the human society and started mimicking people, ruling over them, firstly from the lower dimension, from astral, but soon enough from the physical plane, as well.

It led to the conclusion that further decay must at all costs be stopped, a new beginning must be made, a new human, from the genetics of all the lineages descending from Lyra must be made, and this new human should start from scratch, in order to learn to grow and develop from the basics, to learn to go back to the divine itself through experiencing the consciousness in the human body. This is the true origin of us, modern people.

All phases in the manifestation of the divine consciousness are packed in our body in the form of chakras, so that we can gradually raise the level of our awareness, and our entire being which is the microcosm, we can become conscious of the divine essence and its manifestation into this world. In such a way, *by means of chakras, people are forced to develop through work and they cannot separate their outwardly life and work from the state of their consciousness. Chakras connect consciousness and existence, that is actions. The state of human consciousness while it is still in the body directly reflects human lifestyle, and vice versa.* It was the only way to connect the presence of divine consciousness in existence through humanity ('Kingdom Come' to be made on Earth). Such a consciousness can be realized in humans only, individually and of their own free will, not based on some already acquired knowledge and learning, but only through the individual, always original experience. Divine never imitates or imposes itself, it is known by pure grace, as a result of free will, it is found at the heart, individually, like love and justice.

Therefore, a modern humans was created with the goal of starting from the bottom and going all the way to the top, to God-knowing, through the entire development which includes the material development, the development of science and technology, but through the humans himself. Once again, they are not to do it through the acquired knowledge of their ancestors, or magic, but from within themselves, their own experience and work, to rely on their own effort to learn about science and the secrets of nature. *The meaning of a human's life on this planet is to implement the overall awareness and the return to divine consciousness.* Traces of former glory and civilizations of the ancient past and cosmic knowledge were hidden away and a new chapter in the civilizational growth was set in motion. This breaking point took place about 12.000 years ago.

The Moon was brought to where it is now. Why?

THE INFLUENCE OF THE MOON
ON THE SOUL

Moon is the key force which connects the soul to the body on planet Earth and brings forth the necessary dynamics of oppositions in development. Without the Moon only the consciousness of the soul existed, the solar consciousness, souls were able to incarnate in the physical body consciously, use all the experiences they wanted to experience consciously, and leave the body consciously. Cycles of incarnations did not exist. It was a one-sided activity, without the experience of its own opposition, therefore incomplete, over time it became destructive, and the best case scenario it became incapable of growth. There is no true development that could encompass the entire planet Earth in that scenario.

Life was like this on planet Earth up until 12.000 years B.C. Without its opposition solar consciousness of the soul cannot be aware of itself while it resides in the body in a permanent and harmonious way. Because of one-sidedness over time disturbances and imbalance occurred. That is why the Moon was brought over here so as to be directly synchronized with the Sun with its position and movement. *The Moon enables the balance of oppositions and complete development on planet Earth.*

The Moon functions simply by enhancing the oppositions. Within human, in their body and psyche, and outside of him, by enhancing the male-female polarity, it brings all the temptations in those relationships.

How does the Moon provide us with the opposition so necessary for development? By veiling the solar consciousness making it invisible even to itself; by separating the mind in the body from its ties with the consciousness of the soul; *by attaching the consciousness to the body to such a measure that it forgets its source in the soul and divine consciousness*, the source which connects it to the whole existence.

It was all achieved with the Moon's proportions which are connected with the Earth and Mars. The Moon is about half the size of Mars, and Mars is half that of Earth. The connection with Mars is much needed because our karmic experiences still have their past in connection with Mars. On the Earth (on the Giza plateau), on the Moon (on the dark side) and on Mars (Cydonia) large pyramids exist that are interconnected. The Moon with its proportion, position and movement connects our karmic past from Mars with the present time on Earth thus enabling the harmonious development in the future. Pyramids conduct and connect the consciousness and the frequencies of the lower and the higher dimensions, pyramids are always there where the conscious growth is present, where life is not about harsh reality only.[8]

---

[8] Pyramid is the only geometric shape which transforms the Hertzian frequencies into non-Hertzian (scalar), which binds and harmonizes them. On the top of each pyramid a vertical helix of non-Herzian radiation pointing in the direction of the sky can be measured, from about 28 kHz, several meters in diameter. At the foot of each pyramid a flow of water goes underneath enabling the transition from Hertzian to non-Hertzian frequency. On the nature of Hertzian and non-Hertzian frequencies see my books 'The Physics of Consciousness' and 'Samadhi'. In short, Hertzian frequencies are the ones that constitute the physical universe observable with senses, whereas non-Hertzian frequencies correspond to the higher

Influence of the Moon on the biological life is well-documented. Most living beings have their fertility cycle in direct connection with the Moon and its movement. Plants grow faster when the Moon is waxing. Sea tides, caused by the Moon, regulate the lives of many organisms. Fertility cycles, hormones and bloodstream in our body are all affected by the Moon, our behavior, as well. The expression 'lunatic' refers to the mental state, more precisely mental disorders.

All the influences come from the Moon and they are the way they are due to its sheer size and proximity. The Moon is a gigantic magnet, and the same goes for all the other celestial bodies, too. Its movement around the Earth, as the other magnet in space, induces energy for all the organic life to grow. The overall energy of the organic life is generated by the motion of everything that exists in nature, first and foremost, the rotation of the Earth itself. Energy is the movement of the beings, and the same is true for the movements of all the celestial bodies that have impact on us, they are all magnets of huge proportions. At the base of all the cosmos is electromagnetism.[9] The Earth's movement round the Sun,

---

dimensions that are beyond the physical universe, and correlate with the energy of quantum field or ether. It is represented with the point at the top of the pyramid, and the square base is the physical world in Hertzian frequencies. Nikola Tesla, dr. Nikolai Kozyrev and Dr.Wilhelm Reich (who called it *orgon*) worked with non-Hertzian energy. It is otherwise known as *chi* and *prana*. This frequency operates instantly, irrelevantly of space and time, at speed that exceeds the speed of light. It is at the base of all life. Its existence is hidden and falsified in mainstream science currently taught on universities.

[9] The theory of electric universe is promoted widely by David Talbott and Wallace Thornhil in their books: '*Thunderbolts of the Gods*',

together with all the planets of the solar system, generates life energy we see as organic life by means of magnetic induction. If the Earth stopped moving together with all the other planets, organic life would stop. The Moon is one of the participants of this process of organic life, however since it is the nearest body to the Earth, it plays the biggest part. It, therefore, does not generate life energy it merely has a very powerful influence on its modification.

There is a wrong opinion that the Moon steals our life energy. It steals nothing from us that we have not already given it. It simply has the most powerful effect on us and the way we use our energy.

G. I. Gurdjieff often spoke about the Moon stealing our energy and the fact that our work on ourselves must contain an open fight against the influence of the Moon. However, he stressed that to inspire us to start working on ourselves practically, to awaken and find ways of preserving our energy. If practice were the issue, it is not wrong to assume that the Moon steals our energy. It indeed does so, but there is a wider context to be understood here. If practice were the issue, it is incorrect to present the beginner with the widest context before an individual is ready to understand it. In a similar fashion David Icke in his book: *"Human Race Get Off Your Knees: The Lion Sleeps No More"* puts out true information about the Moon, but comes to the conclusion that it is a massive space ship full of aliens who control us. David Icke deserves all the credits for debunking the lies and conspiracies of the elite, wrongly named 'conspiracy theories', however, he truly lacks the understanding as

---

2005 and *'The Electric Universe'*, 2007. There is also a popular book by Donald E. Scott *'The Electric Sky'*, 2006.

to why conspiracies happen in the first place, what the wider context and the meaning of it all is. In order to understand this, it is necessary to understand the nature of human soul and the purpose of its entering the body.

Nothing in this world can be properly understood without the proper understanding of the human soul and its reincarnation.

Everything that happens in this world, happens because of the human soul.

It is, however, such a powerful divine force that nothing in this world happens without its expressed will. Negative events can only be understood through the correct understanding of the nature of human soul and the nature of this world we are born into, with the understanding the dialectics of their oppositions.

In short, this would be the widest context of the phenomena regarding the Moon and our incarnations in the physical body.

THE POSITION OF THE MOON
IN COSMIC PROPORTIONS

With the arrival of the Moon the Earth lost its status in the cosmic order of proportions of the world creation and in the number of laws that rule the cosmos. The position of the Earth has been upgraded, the conditionality that rules over it has been greatly diminished, the liberties increased and with them the possibility of development.

The science of proportions was brought to us by G.I. Gurdjieff from ancient monasteries of the Middle East, and the detailed explanations of the matter were provided for by his disciple P.D. Ouspensky in his work "*The Cosmology of Man's Possible Evolution*".

According to his teaching the divine Absolute manifested itself progressively through seven phases. Those phases are developed by way of spiral movement (by smashing the Divine hologram) and circling from the higher proportion to the lower one following the law of the golden section. This route is used by the consciousness of existence to descend into the lower states. Every proportion gets its own consciousness of itself and it automatically replicates the original illusion that it is self-sufficient and, by doing so, it creates the next lower proportion, in which the consciousness is more conditioned.

1. Absolute as a whole and the Divine itself. It enables the timeless space which in turn enables every-

thing else. This is the pure being which precedes the consciousness of the Self.

2. All the galaxies. Above them only the space itself that contains them exists. It is the consciousness of the Self as space and the context of all the happenings.

3. All the stars. It is concretized consciousness, in all the possible shapes it can exist. It keeps manifesting as the light of the stars.

4. Our star, the Sun. The consciousness of the lives of human souls on Earth is stored there.

5. Planetary systems around the Sun. It is consciousness of all the aspects of happenings and the dynamics of experiences of human souls on the Earth.

6. The Earth and the organic world on the planet. There the consciousness is identified with the physical life in an individual body, of both plant and animal life alike. There it experiences the karmic drama.

7. The Moon as the Earth's satellite. Consciousness is in the state of sleep or obsession which is a result of the total identification with the body.

This progressive development had to be observed like this, from our point of view, from the Earth, because we cannot look at it from somebody else's imaginary point. This is how it influences us, hence, this is how we observe it. It would be the same from some other point of observation, differences would exist only depending on the proportion the observation is conducted from.

Those are the proportions of existence. Each one has a logic of its own and they cannot mix. The nature of every type of existence can be understood only in the context of proportion it belongs to. Each higher one affects the lower one as the more powerful, but each lower one uses the higher one for its energy or 'food'. For example, the Moon feeds off all organic life on Earth and attracts the life energy of living beings. Although, it is on a scale lower that the Earth, it uses its gravitational pull to attract all the phenomena of the organic world. The Moon affects the organic world the same way pendulum attracts the functioning of the clock mechanism with its movement, the mechanism in this case being the organic life. Naturally, planets of the solar system rule the organic life, but the Moon has the most influence because it is the nearest and the spiral of proportion toward our direction ends there. In a similar fashion the Earth uses the influences of other planets of the solar system, the solar system, in turn, uses galaxy, and so forth.

In each proportion the divine splits itself and forms the Divine of that proportion, always according to the holographic model, into ever smaller entities. Hence, there is Divine that rules all the galaxies, then the stars with all of their planetary systems, as well as, one Divine entity that rules over every planet that can sustain organic life.

Divine consciousness further divides itself into every conscious being that exists in all the worlds.

There is a certain number of laws that rule over each proportion and further condition it.

In the Absolute (1) there is only one law that rules, and that is complete unconditionality.

In all the galaxies (2) three laws rule, the ones that were one in the Absolute, but have now split into three separate ones.

All the stars (3) are ruled by six laws: three received from the higher proportion and three that are the product of the cooperation of these three.

The Sun (4) has twelve laws: three forces ruling the world of the second order add up here, and the six forces ruling the worlds of the third order, plus three forces of the Sun itself.

Planets (5) have twenty-four laws or forces that rule over them: the addition to all the previous ones (3+6+12) and three of their own cooperation, which gives the total of 24.

The Earth (6) is ruled by 48 forces or laws: the sum of all the previous ones (3+6+12+24) and three of its own which are generated as a result of the trinity forces.

Moon is ruled over by 96 laws.

If the Moon had a satellite, it would have 192 laws, and so on.

In this way every lower plane is more conditioned and more dense. The will of the divine Absolute affects directly only the second proportion in line, the third one is already conditioned by the trinity, and all the lower ones keep being conditioned by an ever increasing number of laws and forces.

This should be the explanation as to why the life on planet Earth is like this, hard and conditioned. The Earth is pretty far away from the Divine source and un-conditionality.

However, the Moon has taken on the end point, and thanks to its appearance the Earth is no longer at the end of causality chain. Rendering a more relaxed position for the Earth, it is now a good place for the conscious life to start developing to a much larger degree, with significantly more experiences.

To this entire scale the Moon was added, as counterweight, to bind the consciousness on the Earth much tighter to the physical body, to enable a wealth of experiences. To make it a magnet for the soul. The Earth's

48 laws have additionally been burdened with the Moon's 96. Owing to the Moon, the differentiation of the consciousness on Earth is possible to such an extent that the development from the bottom to the top has been made possible, all the way to the most supreme state - the return to the consciousness of the divine Absolute.

Moon as the counterweight adds more load to the life on earth and more conditioning, but brings bigger and bigger challenges and options, as well. Consciousness in the physical universe grows stronger because challenges are set in its path. The very appearance of the Moon is responsible for the conscious development on the Earth from bottom to top, and for the occurrence of the new, modern human who learns science from the beginning, with no recollection of the ancient past from Lyra and the knowledge of technology previous civilizations were in possession of.

SOLAR AND LUNAR CULTS

The division into the solar and the lunar cults occurred globally in all the religions round about the same time the Moon showed up in our system, 12.000 years ago.

Such division was felt the strongest in ancient Egypt where Seth was connected with the lunar cult, and Osiris with the solar.

All religions are divided into solar and lunar cults. Solar cults are truly spiritual and represent humanity's true nature and its connection with the soul and divine power. A human's higher mind is connected with the light of the sun, with everything that is conscious, life-giving and positive.

Lunar cults, as the opposition, represent human conditionality, mechanicalness, submission to authority. Lunar cults are Islam and Judaism, and the solar cults are esoteric Christianity, Buddhism and all the practices of transcendence (yoga). The Moon controls man's mechanicalness, reflecting the lower consciousness, the feeling of being fenced in one's own senses, the mind and ego, and identification with the body. Man's battle against unconsciousness and mechanicalness is a battle against the influence of the Moon. All lunar cults aspire to use the man's energy and control it, mostly through ethical religions, early commandments and punishments. Solar cults give us energy, they give us methods to increase energy, freedom and consciousness. Lunar cults only offer imitation of true values, in much the same way that the Moon only reflects the light of the Sun. In lunar cults the 'truth' is learnt by heart, it is the same for everyone, and everyone must obey. In solar cults the truth is discovered within, always in a personal and unique way, humans themselves becomes the truth, they radiate it with light and life like the Sun.

INFLUENCES OF THE MOON
IN ASTROPSYCHOLOGY

Astrology is an ancient science which is based on the holographic universe. It practically means that when a certain planet, for example Mars, transits the same spot where many years ago, at the degree of our birth was for example Uranus, we suffer the consequences of this transit, which according to the astrological theory suggests an injury of some kind or energy depletion, depending on the aspects and influences.[10] It is like Uranus was still where it was at the moment of our birth. The theory of the holographic universe explains that every tiny fragment contains within itself a timeless reflection of the whole.[11] It comes close to the discovery of quantum field where everything is timeless, beyond space and time, containing everything that keeps manifesting within the given boundaries of space and time.[12] This is why Uranus still influences us from the place where it was at the moment of our birth. The highest reality is the eternal present. Thus, the consciousness of the present moment is the most creative. Everything is

---

[10] I was an avid student of astrology for over twenty years, I studied it in great detail, and I 'knew' all about it, when I experienced an injury at the exact time when the transit in question of Mars over the natal Uranus happened. Only then did I really learn astrology.

[11] On the holographic paradigm see Michael Talbot's book: *The Holographic Universe,* 1991.

[12] On the universal field in modern physics see the book by Lynne McTaggart: *The Field: The Quest for the Secret Force of the Universe* (2003).

interconnected in the holographic universe because everything is One, the way the true teachings have always taught us.

How has astrology known for thousands of years what the physics only discovers today, is a question for those who negate the alternative history of mankind.

If the movement and functioning of all the planets in the horoscope, we observe like the hands on a clock pointing in the direction of some event, then the movement of the Moon must be seen as the seconds clock hand. It gives the final imprint which determines the moment of a specific event. Depending on the sign, house and aspects of the remaining planets, we can see what event is in question and what area of life it manifests itself in.

The Moon rules the Zodiac sign of Cancer. It is the beginning of summer, period of the year when all life is in full swing, unlike the opposite sign, Capricorn, the beginning of winter, when all life withdraws, from the visible to the invisible. Cancer is the symbol of motherhood and giving birth, childhood, reactions based on emotions and the overall attachment to the emotions and impressions. The Moon affects the body via emotions, our attachment to the emotions is determined by our bodily activities. Giving birth is the most powerful bodily activity determined by our emotions. When a woman becomes a mother she is completely transformed, she has become a new personality, much more than she ever was.

What is important is that the sign of Cancer represents the principle of how souls enter the body, in the process of incarnation. On the other hand, Capricorn is the principle according to which souls overcome the process of incarnation by liberating themselves. This is important to understand how the Moon influences our soul acting like a magnet for our soul. It simply, to the maximum, amplifies and emphasizes everything that is in connection with the physical body so as to keep the soul as strongly identified with the body as possible. Therefore, when we say that the Moon acts like a magnet for our soul, it does not mean it pulls us near, rather it attaches us to the body and corporeal in general.

Since the consciousness of the soul is unobtrusive, in its essence it is nothing but a witness of the overall physical phenomena, it has no interest in itself to attach to a body that is very foreign and incomplete for the soul, only a tiny part of the soul gets incarnated in the body. It is hard for the soul to find any interest to live in this world with the body as limited as this one is. That is why the soul needs help to be forced to enter the body, to get interested in that body and everything that goes on in the world, so as to be able to take part in it. One of the ways to help it achieve this state is the oblivion game the soul plays with itself, and that means forgetting your true nature at the moment of birth, we cannot remember our past lives nor what we were before we were born. If we could remember, we would not participate in the events of this life so whole-heartedly, with zeal and will. We would cheat in the game using memories and the previously gained experience. However, *in order to strengthen the consciousness of the soul on the physical plane it is necessary to implement the new solutions, making decisions and accepting responsibility for them, for the consequences, being creative, and with one's whole being taking part in this creativity*. Consciousness is always unique, repetition negates the consciousness. That is why it is important to have a mind in the body that is attached to it (ego), separate from the consciousness of the soul, but not completely separate, just to have at least a minimal bond with the soul to be inspired to develop and gain higher consciousness. It is necessary that the consciousness in the body acts like it is in it for the first time to be able to function in life. This mind that is of the body and attached to the body is ruled by the Moon.

In Indian philosophy and astrology the common sense or mind, *manas*, is associated with the Moon.

Moon helps the soul to tie to the body and experience all the oppositions the soul itself could otherwise never be able to experience.

More than anything, the Moon achieves this through changeability. Constant change is characterized by the influence of the Moon. This shatters the standard patterns and mental frames of the mind, opening up new possibilities, which the mind itself could never come up with, something which is unknown and new. Forcing us to change all the time, the Moon makes us apply new original solutions and discoveries. This is one of the ways in which we strengthen the consciousness of the soul.

By stimulating change the Moon drives us to strengthen the awareness of what is permanent in us. That what changes all the time is not essential, and this leads us to learn to distinguish that behind all the change we are able to realize what is true and essential and what is not, what is merely transient.

Based on the constant change and temptations that originate from them, the Moon teaches us what the Buddhist philosopher Nagarjuna taught us: that *samsara* and *nirvana* are one, that the highest reality is no different from anything already existing, it is permanent but also present in all the changes, otherwise, it would not be the highest reality. It teaches us to recognize the highest reality in everything that is taking place now, to see the eternal in transient and transient as a part of eternal, to see what is the biggest in smallest. In other words, it reveals to us the holographic nature of the universe, where every piece, no matter how transient, contains the reflection of the timeless whole.

Humans' consciousness of their soul, which is neutral, can easily be influenced via the body, by stressing its needs and functions, especially the ones of the lowest kind, the animal ones. This induces the opposition between the consciousness of the soul and the body in man. However, it is nothing negative, the way some 'spiritual people' often think. Due to this opposition and its constant temptation humans can achieve the true knowing of the consciousness of their soul, its grandeur and significance, but also the true meaning of existence in this world, of the values of this world while they still resides in their physical body. The Moon gives us this. *The true value of something we were born with, the consciousness of the soul, we can only get to know once we lose it and find it again.*

The house in horoscope the Moon occupies determines the area of life where our body is present and exposed to the most. If it is the seventh house, it is something to do with the public, if it is the tenth, the career is important but with constant change, if it is in the ninth, travelling and moving to another country is imminent; if the Moon is found in the twelfth house, the body is in some kind of isolation. Its aspects will deter-mine if it will constructive or destructive action, but all the details depend on the remaining influences of the horoscope which is always viewed as a comprehensive whole.

The Moon affects the body through the primary life feeling, and that is sexuality. Venus and Mars are in charge of romantic life, but *the Moon is the one that determines your sexuality, what you will do with your body*. If your Moon is afflicted by Saturn, in the twelfth house, you will not have a rich sexual life, or you will simply not be interested or you will suffer because you will be deprived these experiences. If it is conjunct with Jupiter, in the eighth house, in Cancer, orgy is the preferred form of sexual satisfaction.

When we speak of the oppositions the Moon provides, we must say that it also provides us with the pleasant feelings, those of the most intense nature. Humans feels they are intoxicated the most with what the position of the Moon brings. It is that strong feeling of bliss in the solar plexus that spreads throughout the whole body, only children can have. It is followed by the feeling of having found one's true sanctuary, the proper home, the right person, the real event. Adult people may experience it, albeit briefly, and it sticks in their mind like the most beautiful moment ever. It is mostly something the body experienced, some carnal pleasure, not a spiritual one. *When we feel and do what fills us with the greatest passion, something that is our obsession – but not spiritual – that is the influence of the Moon.* Its position and interaction with the other planets decides if it will be something positive or destructive, good for us and the people surrounding us, or pure evil. Since these influences come from the unconscious they seem like our own will, which makes it possible for us to commit the most atrocious evil acts as well as the greatest good, we always experience it as our own will and deeper need. There is not a single psychopath out there, or a criminal with a well-placed Moon in his/her chart.

It is a way the Moon ties the soul to the body: with passions that we constantly keep alive by remembering and feeling them, with our imagination, and remaining attached to the past. It is all encouraged by the Moon. At the same time, it is a way for the soul via the body to gain experiences of all sorts of events together with their details in this world. It can only be achieved by having sincere emotions like children do, and the Moon is responsible for that. Emotional maturity and empathy are the main things that enable perception and knowing. Mind is nothing but a scribe and archivist. Therefore, without the Moon, the soul would not be able to experience all the possible details and the meaning of events. ***The Moon has the effect on the soul like a big magnifying glass which enlarges all the details of this world it (astrologically) focuses on.*** Since the Moon is the biggest body in proximity to the Earth it puts emphasis on the sign, house and aspect it makes, which automatically becomes the biggest challenge to man. The Moon simply increases capacity for experiences, it moves the boundaries of perception with its sheer size and power of influence, changeability and inconsistency.

When we speak of the bond of the Moon and the children, childhood and maternity, then we have to explain that all of this lies on the simple fact that the body to a child is the most important and the most immediate means of acquiring experiences and expressing itself in this world. To a mother, the child's body is the most important. To a child, the mother's body is the most important. It is all connected by the Moon's focus on the body regarding the childhood and maternity. The Moon is the largest body to the Earth, and so is the Earth to the Moon.

The Moon affects us through emotions attached to the past and our memories, more specifically, attached to the linear time. The more attached we are to the illusion of linear time, the more we are attached to the illusions of the mind. This attachment also depends on the position of the Moon.

The Moon relates to everything that is unconscious and subconscious. It intensifies the irrational and its phases are connected to such manifestations, from the most cruel crimes based on completely irrational reasons, to the most elevated inspirations. When a person is identified with the body, hence, with the influences of the Moon, he/she will enjoy everything to the fullest. He or she sees that as their own will and desire, always quite justified.

The position and the movement of the Moon indicate that it brightens the dark side of the mind. It reflects the sunlight, never in a uniform manner, but through all the degrees and stages. Sunlight is consciousness, and when the sun sets it vanishes. But there is the Moon which reflects it during the night. It sends out a reflection, diminished but sufficient, on such areas of man's existence the consciousness of the soul could never light up. We receive the influences of the Moon beyond the conscious mind, from the subconsciousness. That is the reason we feel them like our own will making the influences strong and hard to get rid of. That is why this reflected (this phony) light of the Sun's consciousness, we receive via the Moon, can be distorted in millions of ways. If the divine consciousness, which is everything-that-is manifests itself into everything-that-can-be, then those distorted experiences are a part of its intention. Sun can achieve it via the Moon that acts like a mirror. The Moon itself does not do anything wrong there.

In connection with this we can understand why the Moon in astrology is associated with technology, electronics more than anything, the visual media, cameras, why Cancers are the best photographers and cameramen, the best with computers. A picture, a snapshot, a photography is just a reflection of something, it is not really the object itself. The same way moonlight is just a reflection of the sunlight. Technology is also a reflection and consequence of the skill of man's consciousness to act in this world. This skill depends on the influence of the Moon. The same way the Moon magnifies attachment to the body and bodily experiences in general, it like a lens magnifies all the details of nature and its possibilities, where technology fits perfectly: the augmented possibilities of nature. Electronics is greater perception and the functioning of nature down to the level of electron. That is why the Moon (and Cancer) is associated with electronics. Nikola Tesla was born under the horoscope sign of Cancer.

It could be said that people in this world before the appearance of the Moon lived self-sufficient lives without the technological process, they had what they needed for normal living. Due to strong consciousness of their soul the overall existence they clearly saw as divine and perfect and everything was enough for them without the development of technology. But that did not bring the development of civilization. It was all initiated with the appearance of the Moon.

Finally, describing the Moon's influence in astrology cannot be complete if we fail to mention the absence of its influence if it is unaspected, if it does not have any aspects with other planets, which is not good. It is a well-known fact from the astrological practice that it is better for the Moon to have any kind of aspect with any planet in the chart, than none at all (till the final degrees of the sign it occupies), because then the life of such a human is uneventful, uninteresting and monotonous. The Moon greatly affects events and their dynamics. The more the aspects, the more events and experiences there are, and the more opportunity to become aware through all of these experiences.

Still, the absence of the Moon's aspects does not have to be all negative. It has its share of influence, but only through the sign and the house. Decreased influence of the Moon may simply signify the karmic maturity of the soul who is no longer in need of such influences, it finds it easy to get rid of them and focus on the work with other planetary aspects.

LILITH – THE BLACK MOON
THAT, TOO, EXISTS

It seems we have two versions of the Moon, the one we see in the night sky which is intended for the outer growth, the one aimed at the conscious mind. The other version is aimed at the lowest passions and drives, but our talents, as well. Talent is something we have inside, in our subconscious, we are unaware of it up until the point we discover it during the process of working on ourselves. It can be both good and bad. The visible Moon gives us influences which have a collective impact on us and everyone can see them, while the Black Moon gives us influences the conscious mind is unable to detect until it crashes into them, and they are experienced individually.

Astrologers speak of Lilith, the Black Moon, there are even ephemerides for its movement. It was named Lilith who is, according to Talmud, the first, unmarried wife of Adam, who taught him all the secrets of the body and developed his talents and drives his official wife Eve, a housewife and mother, could not teach him.

Lilith is the mother of all demons, hence her influence extends to the dark side of existence which is out of reach of this ordinary Moon even, which is intended for the average man. If the Moon is responsible for the basic instincts, Lilith is the same for the lowest kinds, the ones we would not consciously expect of ourselves or others. If the Moon is a magnifying glass enlarging the drives that chain us to the body, Lilith is the Microscope of the Atomic Forces.

Therefore, we can say that the ordinary Moon is intended for the control of the physical body, and Lilith is for the influence over the astral body. All the influences are covered this way of all the areas humans resides in, during their awakened state (the physical world) and in sleep (astral).

Allegedly, some astronomers claim to have seen it, but there is no official confirmation for this, and it is therefore regarded to be hardly visible. The first sighting was in 1618. by Piccoli, then Cassini in 1672. Clyde Tombaugh, who made the discovery of Pluto, was searching for it for 40 years. The last sighting was in 1926. through a telescope at the Berlin Treptower Park. It is closer than the Moon and rotates round the Earth in 124 days. And it *is not* asteroid classified as 1181 Lilith, a temporary marking 1927 CQ.

In all likelihood, it seems to be some contraption made of glass that rotates round the Earth and has no intention of being seen, but would rather act covertly.

THE MOON
AND THE POLARIZATION OF HUMANS

The opposition the Moon generates, and its attachment to the body, is emphasized and manifested concretely in two sexes in people. In a human being it is the polarity of the hemispheres of the brain, a psychological division into the male and the female principle, into the anima and animus the Jung's psychology speaks of. Male body carries anima within, the female principle, while the female body has an animus within, the male and solar principle. Man's outward appearance seems to have a solar force, but inside he is vulnerable and emotionally dependent on the lunar influence. Woman's outward appearance is vulnerable and gentle, physically under the influence of the Moon, while, at the same time, she has the solar principle inside and is much stronger and more rational than a man.

Because of the strong solar principle in them women are more aware of the consciousness of the soul than men, all the phenomena regarding the spiritual and soul they recognize much better. They carry inside the solar principle, the consciousness of the soul, all they need to do is open up and surrender. Men have to become free (sober up) from the lunar influence in order to recognize it. They must work on themselves in order to reach the consciousness of the soul, the solar principle.

However, it only applies to the ideal state and theory. In practical life everything is mixed up.

On the outward, the Moon has made a much bigger division between the sexes than was the case before the Moon showed up in this world. People were united and far closer, both telepathically and emotionally. But back then, they did not have this dynamics in the male-female relationships the way we have them today, the type of dynamics that by means of tension increases the level of awareness in all the details by which the consciousness of the soul is crystallized in man. The increased consciousness of the soul in humans increases the presence of the divine consciousness and grace among people and on the global scale.

Holographic universe reveals to us by means of astrology how our body is made up of the influences of the signs and planets. Every functional part of the body (legs, hands, hips, neck, head…) reflects the principles of a specific astrological sign and planets ruling those signs. In the male body the right eye is of the Sun and the left one is of the Moon, whereas in women the situation is the other way round, the right eye is of the Moon and the left one is of the Sun.

The appearance of the Moon polarized all the processes on the Earth by speeding up the development of life in all the aspects. For the divine consciousness in humans to become complete, the way it was depicted on the well known symbol of yin-yang in Taoism, the Moon had to show up. With only the solar consciousness that would not have been possible. In the symbol of yin-yang the light field symbolizes the influence of the Sun, and the dark field the lunar influence.

The polarization of the human being is best described by the alchemy through the symbolics of the Sun and the Moon. An ideal of human authenticity and wholeness is achieved by means of conscious unity of humans polarization, its understanding and overcoming, which is symbolically represented as the wedding of the Sun and the Moon in humans with the aid of intelligence, Mercury.

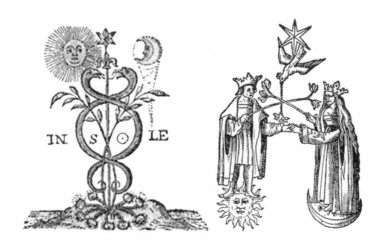

LIBERATION FROM THE INFLUENCE
OF THE MOON

Humans are unaware of their body to a considerable degree, they unconsciously implement with their body all the unconscious contents. Therefore, the Moon exercises easy influence over humans from within their subconsciousness and onto their body. *A method for liberating oneself from the influence of the Moon is based on the awareness of the body.*

The work of G. I. Gurdjieff is based on the man's complete awareness achieved only through practice, and that means through the awareness of the body. The dances he brought over from the ancient monasteries of the East had this purpose. The dances are so complex and intricate that they require complete awareness and control over the body to perform. Not only the control of oneself only, but of all the participants as well, because those dances were practiced in large groups, in a synchronized manner. They are not ballroom dances but methodical exercises of awareness and activation of certain energy centers in the body that raise the level of consciousness.

In a milder and wider context, all forms of human endeavor serve the same purpose. Work raises the level of awareness in humans, forcing them to become conscious of the body and all its abilities, making them control themselves and become aware of their environment.

The more we are aware of ourselves and our body, the less it can be controlled by the Moon.

We set ourselves free from the influence of the Sun each time we resist the desires of the body and its drives and strengthen our will and independence, the objective consciousness which is of the Sun and the soul. That was very nicely put by Sadashiva, a saint mentioned in the famous Swami Yogananda work, *Autobiography of a Yogi*. When asked how he attained his powers (*siddhi*) he replied: Never do what you feel like doing (which comes from the influence of the Moon) and you will be able to do everything you feel like doing (expressing the will of the Sun, its soul).

If we cannot find a group that practices the holy dances of the kind of G. I. Gurdjieff's school, we can much easier find a practice of awareness of the body which is conducted as a part of the Buddhist meditation called *vipassana*. It is a practice of meditation in which the whole being of humans is systematically made aware of: the body and breathing, the feelings, expressing will, and all the way to the mind itself and every single thought. They are all systematically brought to the level of awareness, firstly each activity separately (only the body, only breathing, only feelings...) and then collectively.[13]

All of the ancient spiritual teachings that convey the truth were based on one same principle: humans awareness of themselves, their complete awareness and the practical work on themselves with the end result of objective awareness. All forms of false spirituality offer a lot more theory, convincing and religious ideology in-

---

[13] On the practice of meditation see my book: "*Meditation – The First and the Last Step – From Understanding to Practice*".

stead of practical proof of one's own consciousness. Now it is clear to us why all those false spiritual teachings are under the influence of the lunar cults.

The influence of the Moon can be recognized in everything that attracts us, but is not real or justified. The same way that moonlight is not real, but a mere reflection of the real thing, the same way in which the Moon is unnatural, all its influences are like that. On the other hand such influences can be the road to creativity, accepting the new and unknown, accepting that what the logical mind would never go for.

We are always under the influence of the Moon when we are childish in our behavior, when we indulge our weaknesses and desires, and when they seem irresistible and justified. And when we go on repeating them with no good reason. Solar consciousness of the soul expresses itself in the form of adult, mature and responsible behavior.

Moon plays a great part on the sphere of sexuality. Getting oneself liberated from its influences in sexuality is based on the following understanding. Profound aspiration toward the sexual contact is a tendency to go back to the original unity, orgasm brings bliss because of a short-lived experience of the unity with the whole, at that moment ego and the feeling of separation disappear. That is why orgasm is so appealing. For man a woman's sexual organ is attractive because of the unconscious wish to go back to the mother's source in the blissful safety of his fetal stage, when he unconsciously enjoyed the divine unity. Woman's tenderness he seeks in accordance with the model of motherly tenderness he experienced as a child. In astropsychology the Moon in a male chart represents a woman and a mother at the same time. Woman through sexuality - through union with the opposite sex - wishes to be fulfilled with the wholeness. She looks for the same kind of stability and spiritual safety in humans that she experienced as a child in her father.

This unity is, however, also experienced in the deepest meditation, in *samadhi*, but with the full alertness and tendency to make it a permanent experience, so that we can experience our unity with the divine whole eternally and enjoy it throughout all the daily activities, moderately, not explosively and for a brief moment only.

Unity with the whole can be experienced through the body and independently of the body. In meditation the unity is experienced independently of the body. *The Moon makes us aspire toward this unity only through the bodily experience of the union with the opposite sex, through the ecstasy of the body, orgasm*. It is experienced through the body only in a conditioned way, depending on the contact with the other sex, instantly, therefore, transiently. This transience usually increases the hunger for repetition, where sex is reduced to constant, often needless and excessive repetition, more like addiction, really. This is a way of losing energy, and because of this it is said that the Moon steals our energy. By constant repetition the real purpose of sexuality is lost and the need for satisfaction is easily transferred on to the other perverse forms. Likewise, when a person is deprived this aspiration, and it is not like one can always be perfectly satisfied, conflicts and negativity arise, the innermost, psychological ones, but the outward disorders manifested in communication with people, as well.

It is necessary, however, to experience both experiences of unity in the proper way, through the body, and independently from it. Bodily unity through sexuality is introduction, a preparatory experience that reveals to us a wealth of bodily and physical life in general, giving us the greatest joy in life, during the experience of the sexual union we feel alive the most. That is why all the beauty and joy exists in people. At its base it is always sexual. But those are only spontaneous, instant experiences that require constant repetition and numerous other conditions to be met, all of which are in connection with the interpersonal relationships and the quality of life. The good side is that we are forced to perfect and nurture all of this. In order for the unity with the divine whole, we aspire toward both consciously and unconsciously in all kinds of ways all our lives, to be a permanent experience and become our way of life, we need to experience it independently of the body, through the discipline of meditation, *samadhi*.

We are capable of experiencing the awareness of unity with the divine whole in a variety of ways. Chakras in our body enable this experience. ***With every single chakra we are able to have an orgasm, the unity with the whole***. In the first chakra it is energy union used in all forms of struggle, during physical action, in fights. In the second chakra the exchange of energy with the opposite sex takes place in the sexual union (Moon has its strongest pull there, sex for the sake of sex). In the third chakra it is the accomplishment of a higher goal after sexual union (starting a family, offspring, social goals). In the fourth chakra we experience an orgasm by knowing the unity of energy which is in us and in the whole, a conscious cognition of the overall unity of energy is experienced through the feeling of divine love, then we are in the sexual intercourse with the whole, we love everyone, not just our partner, which is the case in the second chakra. In the second chakra we were able to have sex, in the fourth one we make love, we experience the universal love, not just with the partner but with the entire existence. In the fifth chakra we are finally able to express our awareness of unity with the divine whole, the orgasm in the fifth chakra gives ecstasy of poets and sages who convey the eternal truths to the world. In the sixth chakra we during orgasmic ecstasy experience everything that words or mind cannot begin to express, what the mind cannot see, it is a mystical experience in which the energy of existence is seen like the divine light (aura) of life. In the seventh chakra we are permanently united with the divine whole, in a permanent bliss, compared to which the experience of orgasm in the second chakra looks like child play and illusion.

In the first three chakras we experienced the consciousness of unity under the influence of the Moon, illusory, conditioned and changeable. In the fifth, sixth and seventh chakra the unity with the divine we get to accomplish under the influence of the Sun, the eternal light of the stars.

Consequently, it may become a little clearer to us how much better it is to outgrow the influence of the Moon and the lower three chakras. The biggest illusion the Moon provides for us is that we stand to lose something if we overcome its attractive influences through the experience of the body. Quite the contrary, we only stand to gain so much more. With the full consciousness of the soul we see in the very body the divine presence we naturally aspire to in all ways possible. Without such consciousness we may even decline to inhumanity. This lunar illusion equals nonsense that we should forever remain in childhood, playing with toys, with our own body. Adulthood, world and life offer far bigger potentials for playing and more luscious enjoyment. The entire cosmos.

The influence of the Moon can be overcome by strengthening the solar consciousness. We can receive it in a number of ways, one of which is directly, via the sun. Sun with its photons and ultraviolet light (UV) sends information on to us for the functioning of DNA via pituitary gland which is directly linked to the eyes. Sun's radiation is of informative nature, it enables the overall life with its data. When we say that the Sun is the source of all life we should know what it means. Information the living beings receive from the Sun is similar to those the musicians get from the conductor, they harmonize life, cleanse it of rejects, synchronize well all the phenomena. For the spiritual growth and releasement of all the weaknesses induced by the Moon, apart from meditation, it is always a good idea to practice solar yoga, looking at the Sun, according to the instructions of Hira Ratan Manek and the advanced course of solar yoga according to the instructions of Sunyogi Umashankar.

The final point of understanding the key moment when we are untied from the influence of the Moon is in the following.

The reason we as souls decide to incarnate in the human body during which process we forget the larger part of our true nature, the divine nature, is for us to become aware of our divine nature in our physical bodies, during our lifetime, and ground this divine consciousness to the earth as a legitimate experience, on to the physical plane. Once that is accomplished the divine consciousness is complete in all the aspects of its existence, it reveals itself to us as the existence itself. More accurately, such a human reveals to the world that divine consciousness is existence in itself, it is everything-that-is and everything-that-can-be.

The Moon has assisted the consciousness in the body throughout its journey in this world, with all the oppositions involved. On other planets, where there is no Moon like this, souls also go through experiences, but in a much poorer way than we do. Only on this planet is it possible, for example, that at the same time you love God, your dog and your spouse, and after about a month you start to hate them. Such a wealth of choices to be made and numerous possibilities do not exist on other planets. Be aware of it at all times and enjoy your life on this Earth.

The key moments in the maturing of consciousness of the soul in this world are those instances where we make our own decisions based on our conscience, or the bond of our physical mind with the higher consciousness of the soul. Those are always decisions that we will no longer follow, the impulses of the body and the lower mind, its mechanical habitual actions, repetitions and conditioning, but we will choose to be responsible for a higher goal and purpose, by making a turning toward what is permanent in us. It is basically making a choice between the good and evil.

The only permanent thing about us is the solar consciousness of our soul. Everything that is changeable and conditioning falls under the category of the Moon's influences. In reality, that is the key difference between the solar and the lunar consciousness. It is not only the phases of the Moon that affect the body, but the body itself is as changeable as the Moon. In about a month almost the entire body changes, we get new skin, blood, most of the cells in the body. It is therefore easy for us to distinguish between the consciousness of our soul which is our permanent essence and is above the body, and the physical body that keeps changing completely and perpetually like the Moon.

When we succumb to the Moon's influences it is like sledding down on the toboggan following the line of the least resistance. All the power of the lower mind serves the purpose of justifying it in all possible ways, if the mind is incapable of doing so by itself, then with the help of alcohol and lower instincts.

Anyone who has ever hurt themselves or anybody else, or committed a crime, did so under the influence of the Moon, depending on its position in the horoscope. They definitely were not under the influence of the solar consciousness of their soul. They were obsessed with something that is transient in nature, and conditioned with who knows what, but due to the narrow consciousness it looked so inevitable and fateful, so life-changing, that something 'had be done with it'. That is the way in which the influences of the Moon operate, they narrow the consciousness to what is happening at the moment only and turning it into the highest reality. That is why it is so hard to resist it. The solution to situations like these is 'to sleep on it', not to act out, be impulsive and rash, one should wait for at least 24 hours and allow themselves to react then, if there still is need.

The Moon narrows and conditions our consciousness based on one regularity of our mind, and that is its propensity to split, it is not unanimous. We have a multitude of I's that shift intermittently, so that we have an illusion that we have only one I. Only when this 'one' I becomes contradictory to itself, starts to do what it wants, forgets and breaks its decisions, we appear to be at a loss. The answer is simple: we have a myriad of split

I's, multiple minds that shift but invisibly to us up until the moment when we crash into something with our inconsistency or some harder consequence. The multitude of I's corresponds to the phases of the Moon, a multitude of Moon's faces, it keeps changing all the time, it is never the same.

There is an important regularity in connection with the liberation from the influences of the Moon.

If we want to get rid of some habit and mental pattern that restricted and had a negative influence on us, *if we manage to resist it during one full lunar cycle, then we will forever set ourselves free from that weakness and habit*. This works for everything whether it is smoking, drug addiction, sexual addiction, financial failure, implementation of the law of attraction. If we manage to detach ourselves from this for the duration of the Moon's cycle of 28 days, if we manage to dissociate from it mentally and physically, then we will succeed permanently. The permanent attachment will vanish, and at least there will be no influence from the Moon. Humans are always free to go back to their old habits and ways, but then it will only be because they have not managed to detach with their whole being, but they left an open door in the subconscious to go back in to their old ways some day. In other words, they were playing a game with the split mind, one part renounced the bad old habit, and the other one was just waiting for it to end to be able to go back to the way things were before. Actually, it is enough to succeed for the period of 21 days, the remaining time is a test and establishing the change. Basically, what happens during that time is our effort to attain one whole "I", unanimous, our own will. If we manage to persevere for the full 28 days there are no longer any obstacles in the path of our liberation. The question is only whether we were and are complete within ourselves to see the whole matter through.

The choice between the Moon and the Sun in us is the choice between the bodily and spiritual, childish immaturity and eternal wisdom, between the transient and low and permanent and sublime, between silly and serious, strong and weak, collective opinions and individual ones, between the wide road paved with good intentions leading to demise, and a road less-traveled, a narrow passage leading to salvation.

Always when we strengthen our will with which we fight off weaknesses that tie us to our illusions of the past we have detached ourselves from the influence of the Moon.

Strengthening our will does not mean wasting our energy on what the Moon keeps conditioning us, on the illusions and transient wishes, but on permanent values that are in the best interest of the real life and well-being. It is said that the Moon steals our energy, it feeds off it, but that actually means that we distribute our energy on the needless and transient things. It is easy to detect them because they are always about repetition, habits, obsessions connected with the senses and physicality, and they are all illusory.

However, it does not mean that we should be negative toward anything, including the influences of the Moon. The old alchemists pointed in the direction of the holy marriage between oppositions in humans represented in the form of the Sun and the Moon, male and female nature in us. Only by understanding both influences can we overcome all the negativity of the lunar influences. Understanding brings transcendence, it reveals the transcendental consciousness of our soul. Soul is transcendental by nature in relation to the body and that means it does not affirm itself with any negation or resistance toward anything, but only through understanding with which the ignorance is overcome. When the existence we observe with the consciousness of the soul makes us realize that at the foundation of the body and the entire existence there is only the divine consciousness, we see that nothing but the divine consciousness exists. Therefore, the problem was never the Moon but our lack of understanding and ignorance. It is like the moonlight, illusory, transient and changeable.

According to the experiences of clinical death and hypnotic regression into the past lives, when humans leaves this world they recapitulate their entire life and experiences not only the things they did to others, but how the others experienced it and what that did to them. Hence, they view everything from both sides, both subjectively and objectively. This experience is the reason why the soul makes a decision to be born again: to correct its mistakes ('sins') and continue the process of becoming aware in the body. However, the cycle of incarnations carries on until such maturity of consciousness of the soul and emotional maturity is achieved during the life in the physical body, that they have become fully conscious of this experience here and now in this life. An emotionally mature human, with conscience and consciousness of the soul, cannot do anything wrong to another being because they feel directly how the other party experiences that. With such awareness humans know from within all by themselves what the right thing to do is. Then they have attained the divine consciousness in the body and no longer need incarnations.

Moon helps by reflecting the consciousness of the Sun onto the darkness of our life. It enables our vision at night, in the dark of our physical world. By doing so it widens the range of consciousness and assists development on the physical plane, it increases emotional maturity with which we become aware of everything we do in this world.

Liberating oneself from the influences of the Moon is the basis for all the ethical codes and behavioral norms in all the religions and all the societies. Everywhere the idea of culture is knowing how to act within the limitations of one's body, what to do in every situation, what kind of behavior is acceptable and proper and what is not. Traditions are based on experience and they decide what kind of behavior is right and beneficial for the survival of community life. Every ethical and moral code that regulates the conduct of individuals within the community is one of the ways of outgrowing the influence of the Moon. The Moon drives us to behave in an instinctive, impulsive and unconscious manner, based on the acquired impressions and habits, and not based on the objective need in accordance with reality. With the influences of the Moon our consciousness is always narrowed, focused on what is contemporary but transient, with the solar influences our consciousness gains a far better perspective and rises toward that of the permanent value.

However, ethics and morality can never cover all the individual aspects of behavior and the needs of people, they are based on collective interests and the minimum which enables the survival of the community, often at the expense of freedom of the individual. Far better and stronger than all the ethical teachings and morality, the practice of meditation helps untie us from the influence of the Moon. We go through the direct experience of our true identity, we become aware of the fact that we are not our body, we are so much more, we are the eternal transcendental consciousness of the soul. When even for a brief moment we experience this during meditative focus, in *samadhi*, then we experience that consciousness of our soul is the same divine consciousness that enabled and manifested everything that exists. We, then, experience the body as a temporary, albeit useful means for the manifestation of divine consciousness in this world and then it can no longer distract us with its childish urges and inferior passions. Then, the body does not trap us any more; we use it, it does not use us.

AND FINALLY,
WHO FRAMED US WITH THE MOON

Now when we know everything about the Moon, that it is an artificial creation, and we are well-equipped with information coming from the sphere of science on this subject, how do we feel about the people who walk down the street not paying much attention to the Moon, not looking for the truth in it because they think it is natural, same as everything else? We should consider their walking as a form of sleepwalking. They are not drawn to take an interest in the Moon, they watch their mobile phones and think that something which is not real, which is nothing but a reflection of something, is actually for real. This is how the mirror of the lunar mind functions.

However, it is not all that bad, this world with people who resemble zombies, does not have to look like a cosmic prison for the feeble-minded, the way some conspiracy theorists claim so wrongly, because nothing is hidden away from man. Everything is right before their eyes; only they do not see it, and it only depends on them whether or not they decide to see it. It would be a lot more scary if all of that was completely covert, if we did not have a possibility even to liberate ourselves from the identification which makes us mechanical and unconscious, conditioned in so many ways.

Knowing the truth and freedom are readily available for us and before our very eyes, although we are under no obligation to see it, and instead choose to enslave ourselves further. Even though we can kill ourselves in the darkness of our illusions, we always have the freedom to enlighten ourselves. Is that wonderful, or what?

Only the strength of our consciousness determines what we choose to see and whether we bother to see it, at all. There is no other way for the consciousness of the soul to crystallize, become strong and express itself, but through us, the way that has been explained on the pages of this book. It is poetic justice.

The magnitude of the Moon and this entire project that goes along with it, the amount of intelligence invested, work and resources, show that we are worth it. If all of this were done for us, we must be worth it, our power is worthy of it.

In the end we can fast forward this issue and reveal the obvious:

Our soul placed the Moon to be able to incarnate and experience all the aspects of divine existence.

Without it, the soul would also incarnate but then the pace of life and development would be a lot slower and self-sufficient. If there were no Moon, we would live like we did 12.000 years ago. Ok, maybe like 500 years ago. The appearance of the Moon greatly enhanced the karmic maturity and material development on this planet. The Moon was placed by very advanced alien forces, but in the holographic universe we are all one. *We are the 'aliens' who did it, although not in our current bodies. They are our older versions*. Its astrological influence, its position in our horoscope, is not by accident because it like a mirror reflects the karmic maturity of our soul in this incarnation, the contents of experiences we should experience, that bring us one step closer to us, to our consciousness. *The Moon serves us, not the other way round.*

There are indeed so many things we did with the divine power of the creative consciousness of our soul, before we were born in these bodies of ours.

If you could observe things now with the consciousness of your soul you would be able to see that the entire cosmos, life and absolutely everything that exists and happens – is a concrete physical reflection of the consciousness of your soul, the reflection of your divine consciousness.

The Sun and the Moon every day and night show this from the sky as clear as could be.

Still, people do not see that – because the Moon is so good at its job.

Made in the USA
Las Vegas, NV
10 March 2021